EXCELLENT CUSTOMER SERVICE

How to Build a Customer Service Culture in a Retail Environment

By

EJ Bones

EXCELLENT CUSTOMER SERVICE

How to Build a Customer Service Culture
In a Retail Environment

Published by EJ Bones
Copyright © 2013 by EJ Bones
Cover Art by EJ Bones

First printing August 2013
First edition August 2013

Intro

What exactly are we talking about when we say we want to build a culture which provides customers with excellent customer service? What does it even mean? Let's start with how we define the very words that we are trying to create.

EXCELLENT - ex·cel·lent [ek-suh-luhnt] possessing outstanding quality or superior merit; remarkably good.

Outstanding! Superior! Excellent means to be beyond the normal expectation. Excellent means that we are raising the bar. Anybody can just provide service. Anybody can open the door to a business and invite people to come in and give them money.

Excellent means that you're beyond 'just being there'. You're above all the rest! You are superior! You consistently rank above all others when it comes to the kind of service you provide your customers!

CUSTOMER - cus·tom·er [kuhs-tuh-mer] a person who purchases goods or services from another; buyer; patron.

These are the people we want. The ones that come into the establishment every day and are trying to give us money! Without the customer the business will cease to exist. The very survival of the business depends on the customer giving the business their hard earned money. Without the customer nothing else that we do will matter. Every single aspect of what a business does every single day should positively contribute to the people that are trying to give that business their money. They are the very center of the business' universe. And every single person working in the establishment needs to believe, breathe and live it!

SERVICE - serv·ice [sur-vis] an act of helpful activity; help; aid: to do someone a service.

Help? Helping customers is what we're supposed to be doing? How on earth can we help them? Help is a pretty broad term if we think about it. Helping can be anything that influences a customer's decision to give us their money isn't it? So what is it that we expect from the front line of employees that support the mission of the company? We expect them to be superior! We expect them to deliver whatever our promises are! We expect them to have a genuine interest in the customer's experience! And we expect them to consistently provide excellent service to our customers! But how are you going to get them to do that?

CULTURE - cul·tur [kuhl-cher] the behaviors and beliefs characteristic of a particular group.

This is the ultimate goal right? We want our entire group of employees to have the same characteristics. We want the entire group of employees to deliver the same results. We want them to be a cohesive unit. In order to have a culture a business must have consistency. A culture doesn't mean that you are chasing after service issues with your customers on a daily basis. A culture doesn't mean that you are receiving complaint after complaint from unsatisfied customers. A culture means that you are nailing it! You have a team of experts working for you and they genuinely believe that what they do every single day contributes to the success of your business, through the service that they provide the customers. They don't even have to think about it. It is their nature. They just do it!

This book is your guide. This book will teach you how to provide your customers with the service you desire. You will build a culture within your establishment. The culture will provide your customers with excellent customer service on a consistent basis. Every single day, every single employee will provide your customers with excellent customer service! Let's begin.

Chapter One

Hiring the team of experts!

The first step in building a strong customer service culture is hiring the right people. The team that you put together needs to be able to deliver your customer service results. They are the ones that you will need to rely on every single shift that they work. They are the ones that you are putting on stage to represent the company and you to your customer. You are hiring people that you will need to have confidence in.

The first step in hiring the right people is gathering. You need applicants. How are you gathering applications? The easiest and most reliable way to gather applications is to have a host site gather and directly email applications to your business. The majority of people applying for jobs will search through the internet for company openings. This is the most convenient method for not only the applicant but also for the company seeking applicants. Take advantage of these methods and save yourself a lot of time.

There are also the tried and true applicants that will walk right through the front door of your business and ask to speak to the manager. As the manager of the business, you need to view these individuals as the cream of the crop. You need to stop what you are doing and take a minute to greet these individuals. You should not view these people as an interruption of your day. These are the people that are putting in the extra effort to find a job. They have more than likely created a resume, gotten dressed up, and rehearsed what they are going to say to you. They are already in effect putting themselves up on the stage to represent you and the company. Show some appreciation and screen them. As you are shaking their hands and thanking them for coming into the establishment ask them a couple of questions. This is your chance to screen the applicant. If you like how they respond put their application in the 'call for an interview' pile.

You may have to work to get quality applicants, however. Do whatever it takes! Hold a job fair, announce to your team that you're hiring (word of mouth goes a long way), partner with corporate friends, present a table at the entrance to the business, and just get yourself a pile of applications so you can build your team! Not every location is blessed with quality applicants so you may need to get creative! The more applications you have to choose from the more specific you will be able to be when you review potential candidates. If you are hiring twenty associates you may want to have one-hundred or more applications. If you are only hiring two associates then ten applications may be enough. Not everybody will make it through the process. You are going to need extras.

Once you have gathered a decent number of applications it is time to review them. This is an important step because you can save yourself hours and hours of time on wasted interviews. You need to be efficient. If you spend too much time on the interview process you will ultimately lower your expectations, just to get through the process, and you will hire the undesirables. Don't make this rookie mistake. Determine what you are looking for in your applicants. Choose three 'must haves' and look for that when you are reviewing the applications. If the applicant doesn't have all three 'must haves' then don't bother interviewing them. Stick to your guns on this one! There should not be any compromising in the review process.

Your three 'must haves' should all impact customer service. You are building your customer service team. Focus! Here are three strongly encouraged 'must haves':

1. Experience. Has the applicant ever spoken to a customer? Do they have an inkling of an understanding of what a customer is? If you are hiring people to deliver your culture and they have never even spoken to a customer, then they shouldn't get the interview. If your applicant has only held positions that were behind the scenes, there may be a reason. The

applicant might be the best car detailer that the world has ever known but they can't formulate a proper sentence when speaking to complete strangers about signing up for a company credit card. Is this the person you are putting on stage to represent you? Probably not! Look for people that have an understanding. Look for people that already have some of the building blocks in place. Look for people that you can have confidence in. There will always be a candidate out there who is exception but just hasn't held the right position yet. But finding that exception means you're taking a gamble. Unless you have an unlimited amount of money to invest in that exception and an unlimited amount of time to look for that exception, don't take the chance. Hire people

11

that you know will be able to deliver customer service!

2. Availability. Is the applicant available to work during the busiest times of the week? If the busiest day of your week is Saturday between ten in the morning and six in the evening, but your applicant is only available Monday through Thursday from six in the evening until ten, don't hire them. Hiring and training is very expensive. You are running a business, after all. Don't invest your money, or the company's money, in people that will not be available to deliver your culture to the masses. If you are looking for people to work an average of twenty hours each week, make sure your applicants are available to work that number of hours. Piecing together a schedule

with people that can only give you one shift each week makes no business sense whatsoever. You will be spending two or three times the amount of money necessary to build your team. And even more importantly, you will be spending two or three times the amount of time necessary to deliver your culture. You will need your people available to interact with your customer, when your customer is there. Build your team with individuals that can work!

3. Commitment. Has your applicant been able to hold a job? Have they held positions for companies for longer than three months? If an applicant has tons of experience with dozens of companies and they have open availability, but they've never stayed with a company for longer

than thirty days, there is probably a reason!

You need to be critical and ask yourself why

this person didn't commit to the company that

invested time and money in them. Are you

looking to repeat the hiring process every thirty

days, or are you looking to build a team that is

committed to delivering your customer service

culture throughout the year? You are investing.

You are giving applicants an opportunity to

work and make money in an environment that

is committed to them as your customer service

representative. Make sure the commitment

goes two ways! They need to commit to you

and your company. They need to commit to

your customer!

Now that you've gathered the applications and

reviewed them, you will need to contact applicants

for a scheduled interview. This telephone call can be used for not only scheduling an interview but also for a quick screening. When the candidate answers the call you have an opportunity to ask a couple of quick questions and the responses you receive can help you finalize your decision to schedule an interview. You may determine that although the application is strong, the candidate will not deliver results. On the contrary you may confirm your decision to schedule them for an interview, which you will immediately do before you hang up the phone. Ask the applicant two questions:

1. Why are you interested in joining our team? Maybe the candidate says, "I love your store and have been a committed customer for years!" This is a good response! They not only have experience with customer service

(you already determined that in the review process) but they are familiar with your environment. If your candidate stutters and says, "I need a job," they might not be the best person to invest in. They want money but are not particularly interested in your company or your customer. Your response should be something like, *"We are in the process of reviewing applications still. I'm glad I was able to connect with you today. We'll be in touch if we decide to schedule you for an interview. Have a good day."*

2. "Tell me in your own words what customer service is?" This is a great question! The answer can be anywhere from a quick but confident description in two sentences or less, to an entire seminar. Hopefully the response

you get is somewhere in the middle; you don't have time to attend the seminar. Your candidate might say, "Customer service is everything that impacts a customer's decision to spend money with us. It is the most important aspect of what we do every single day and we need to appreciate that. Without customers we would cease to exist. We need to ensure that customers are satisfied, happy, and will not only return but they will tell all of their friends how amazing we are!" That would sell me! Or they might say "customer service is serving your customer." If the latter is the case, skip directly to your 'we'll let you know' speech. Otherwise, schedule the interview.

When you are scheduling the interviews be efficient with your time. There's much to be said for scheduling group interviews. You will be able to interview a handful of people within the same block of time. You will be telling your candidates that there is competition for the position. And in telling them that many are seeking the position, they will probably figure out that they are replaceable. There are lots of candidates out there and they are sitting next to three, four or five of them during the interview. It is a big deal to work for you and your company. They need to bring it!

As the interviewer, you need to be organized and professional. This is the first glimpse that the candidates have of your company and the environment that you portray. Make the impression on them that you expect them to make to your customers. Be ready! Be on time! Be respectful! Be a professional!   As the hiring manager you will need to show the candidates that they are important to your success. You understand the importance of a customer service culture because you understand that company associates are internal customers! Treat them that way. Show them that you are ready to interview them. Show them that they are the most important thing you have scheduled during that thirty minute block of time. Show them that you understand the importance of respecting company associates. Give them what you want them to give to you and the company every single day. First impressions go a long way and this is their first one of you and the company.

As your candidates arrive for their interview you should be observing and already taking notes. Before the candidates even open their mouth they have already given you information about who they are and the type of associate they potentially would be. The two 'things' that your candidates are telling you through their actions:

1. Will they have time and attendance issues? If your candidates arrived ten minutes early and are patiently waiting in the break-room for the interview, it's a good sign. If your candidate arrives just in the nick of time or LATE, don't take a chance with them. Grant it there can always be unforeseen circumstances that caused them to be late for an interview but it is a gamble to hire this candidate. Do you want to be running a cash register when you should be managing the environment because they repeatedly cannot show up for their shifts on

time? Probably not. The candidate that does not respect your schedule and the other candidates that are waiting for them to arrive will absolutely not respect your customer.

2. Do they understand the importance of the dress code? One would hope that an interview candidate took one minute of their time to realize what your dress code is. They should arrive for the interview looking like they are ready to play the part. If your dress code is business casual, they should at the very least present that to you and your company for the interview. If they go above and beyond that and show up in a shirt and tie or a business dress it's even better. But if your candidate shows up for the interview looking like they just sped across town from the beach or public

pool then they should not get the job. The role you are hiring for is the role that you are presenting to your customer. The candidate needs to present themselves in a manner that is fitting for the position you are filling.

Part of your job, as you begin to conduct the interviews, is to explain to the candidates how the process works. Let them know how long they will be there. Tell them how you will make sure that they each have a chance to answer a question first. Give them advance notice that you will let them all ask a question at the end of the interview. And explain to them what happens after they leave.

Give them some detail about the position they are applying for. And let them know what their titles will be, should they be chosen to join your company.

Their title should be what you expect them to deliver.

These candidates are potentially your new

CUSTOMER SERVICE ASSOCIATES! Or maybe

they will be your CUSTOMER SERVICE

EXPERTS. Call them what you want them to be. If

you expect them to deliver and be a part of your

culture why would you call them 'cashiers' or 'sales

floor associates'? You can schedule them in different

areas of the store such as the POS station, specific

departments on the selling floor, or at the return desk

but they all need to be CUSTOMER SERVICE

ASSOCIATES. If you are building a customer

service culture in your business, you will want to

deliver the message from the second you offer

employment. And the message your candidates are

hoping to hear by the end of the interview process is,

"Congratulations on becoming one of our Customer Service Associates!"

The questions you ask your candidates should ALL focus on customer service. The interview doesn't have to be extensive but should offer you some insight as to how the applicant will treat your customers. Your process can be brief if your questions are direct. Here is a sample of customer oriented interview questions for a six candidate group interview:

1.   Why do you want to work for us? You may have already asked this question but it is okay to ask it again. The candidate is not on the telephone with you. You can read a lot from a face to face conversation. The personality you see is the personality that will be directed right at your customer. What are you hoping to

see? Look for their energy, positive expressions, and enthusiasm.

2. Give me an example of a time that you provided excellent customer service? This is a great question! Not only will you be able to tell if your candidates understand what customer service is but you will also be able to judge their enthusiasm for customer service. If they are smiling and bouncing up and down in their chair when they tell their story it's a great sign! You want your team members to be engaged to customer service. You want them to be excited about how they can and will positively impact your customer. Remember, these are the people that you are putting on stage!   If your candidate struggles to tell you a story of how they provided

excellent customer service, it's a very bad sign. If they give you an answer such as, "I always smile," and that's the end of the story it's not a good sign either. Smiling is good but is it excellent? Imagine that the stage you put your candidates on is not only for your customers but also for the CEO of the company that you work for. And the candidate stands there silently and smiles. Are you proud? Have you delivered the culture of customer service? Probably not; don't hire this candidate.

3. Tell me how you feel about solicitation? Nearly every company on the planet expects their associates to solicit customers for rewards cards, email addresses, or credit cards. Every single associate that you hire

will need to consistently solicit customers, one hundred percent of the time! Your candidate should understand that solicitation is a part of customer service. Solicitation is the best marketing tool today's companies have. It provides customers information about the company, savings coupons, or announcements of upcoming sales. It offers companies unlimited means of reaching their customers and it keeps them coming back to the establishment. If the candidate rolls their eyes and talks about solicitation as an interruption of their life, it's a very bad sign. If they are uncomfortable with solicitation at all do NOT hire them. There should be absolutely NO exception to this.

4. What frustrates you? Hopefully the responses to this are minimal. Hopefully the person in front of you handles frustrating 'things' well. If this is the question that your candidates spend the most time on, it's not a good sign. If your candidate gives you multiple examples of multiple situations there's a problem. You probably need your team to be able to handle a busy environment, handle delivering results, handle multi-tasking and handle shifting gears if necessary. If the examples you hear fall into the categories you need them to be able to handle then don't hire them.

5. Tell me about a time when you had to deal with an upset customer? Again, you are looking for some depth. You are asking your

candidate to explain their thinking, when faced with a difficult customer service situation. You don't want to hire people that blow this situation off and move on to the next customer in line. They should tell you that they worked to resolve the situation or they got help from the management team. They should be responding positively to this question because they truly understand that every single customer is important. There should be a happy ending to their story. If the only enthusiasm you hear in the candidate's story is when they are describing how crazy their customer was, it's a very bad sign!

6. Tell me about a time that you were a member of a team? You are looking for a story with this question. You are looking for an answer

that will tell you if your candidates work well with others. Will your candidates get along with people that you've already got on staff? Are they going to get along well with your customers? You will get quite a bit of insight from how the candidate answers this question. If they give you an answer that includes results, it's a good sign. They will be showing you that they are proud. They are therefore showing you that they were engaged to what the team was able to accomplish together. They are showing you that success is important to them. If they use the word 'we' throughout their description it's another good sign. They are showing you that they understand how working together as a team will build a culture and together the team will deliver the results. On the flip side, if the candidate tells you that they played pee-wee football when they were six years old, it's probably not a good sign!

The last thing you should do during the interview is offer the candidates an opportunity to ask you a question. Hopefully you get some good questions such as, "are their opportunities for advancement with your company?" This will show you that they are interested in growing their roots with your company. This will show you that they are willing to engage to your culture and commit themselves to the success of the company. On the contrary, if you offer them a chance to ask questions and they just shrug their shoulders, giggle and say "I don't know," you may want to reconsider an offer to hire.

Congratulations! You have completed the interviews! Thank your candidates for coming in and assure them that you will be in touch once your decisions have been made to offer positions with the company.

You should have already determined through the interview process who you want to offer positions to. You may want to review your notes and ratings; there's nothing wrong with double checking. If you are on the fence with any of the candidates however, don't make the offer. You are investing in your service culture and you need to be confident in your candidates. If you are unsure, don't risk damage to your customers, the existing team, and the environment that you provide to both.

Be sure to contact the candidates that you are not going to hire. There's nothing worse for people that have tried to get the job and have participated in the interview process, to never hear a single word back from you. And it's not professional. Call the people that didn't get the job! Thank them for participating. Be a professional. *"I want to thank you for participating in our interview process. I regret that I'm unable to offer you a position with our company. I want to wish you the best of luck in your job search. Have a good day and thank you again."* It's that simple! And now you can move on to the candidates that you are offering positions.

Be enthusiastic! Let them know you can't wait for them to start their new role! Recognize them and congratulate them on doing a good job! This is your first opportunity to show them that you reward good performance. If you come across like it's no big deal and you don't really care, then how is it you are going to expect them to be excited about your customers? If you don't care why should they?

Schedule your new Customer Service Associates for an orientation! Be prepared for the phone call with your new associate. Impress them that you are an organized and professional manager. They don't know anything about the company yet and you are still trying to ensure that they understand the importance of both the environment and their new role. Make sure to let them know how long the orientation will take, remind them about the dress-code and tell them what they will need to bring. If there's parking restrictions for employees tell them where to park. Tell them who will be conducting the orientation so they know who to ask for when they arrive. Congratulate them a second time and tell them that you look forward to working with them!

Chapter Two

The Orientation is the Over View

The orientation is the first day of training. You will want to schedule your new Customer Service Associates for at least a three hour shift. One hour should be spent on new hire paperwork. Another hour can be used for whatever training video or on-line training module you provide. But that leaves you with an entire hour during which you can ensure that your bright and shiny new stars are getting introduced to your customer service culture! Make the most of it!

As your new team members file in for their first day on the job make them comfortable. Let them know that they officially belong with the team. Have a locker ready for them so they can comfortably store their belongings. They are at work now so have them punch in for duty! Let them know how important they are by showing them that you are ready for them to be there. There's nothing worse than showing up for a new job and having to hide your belongings in the corner of the manager's office because they were not prepared for you to be there. You need to be prepared and you need to make them feel welcome.

As you sit your members down for the arduous task of filling out new hire paperwork, take some time to introduce them to the company. Tell them a little bit about who you are and how the role that they play impacts your business. Talk about customer service! Tell them what it means to provide excellent customer service. At this point in the training you need to speak in general terms but you need to speak about it! If you have hired these people to deliver the customer service results you desire and you're not making it a part of their orientation, then you are dropping the ball. Don't drop the ball!

Your introduction speech should be something like this:

"Welcome to our company! I want to congratulate you all on becoming new members of our customer service team! We are committed to providing our customers with excellent service. Everything you do as a customer service associate will positively impact our customers. We take pride in the service we provide and we are thrilled to have you join our team! Let's get some paperwork filled out, so we can begin your exciting new career!"

Short, sweet and to the point. The team you have hired needs to hear how important the culture is and they need to hear it throughout the entire hiring and training process.

After the paperwork is complete comes the tour! Bring your team through the building and show them where they will be working. And as you are showing them around, you need to be speaking about customer service!

Be organized throughout the tour. The entire tour should not take more than an hour but needs to be thorough. Within the hour that you have left with your new Customer Service Associates, you will want to show them certain areas of the store that are important to you culture. There are areas of the store that you MUST include. Organize your time so the tour is efficient. You don't want your new employees exhausted by the time you've finished showing them the building that they work in. The tour can be organized into your top five MUST shows:

1. **The Training Room**

    You're probably already in the training room or office area, because you've just completed the paperwork with your new customer service associates. Start where you are:

    "This is our training area/room! We are committed to providing our employees with training that is necessary and specific to the jobs that they do. Every person that works here will have customer service training. Customers are the reason we are all here and we ensure that each employee is provided with the tools that will help them deliver excellent service to our customers."

2. **The Break-room**

In your break-room there are probably bulletin boards, notices, announcements, and maybe the schedule. Show your new associate all of these things. Explain to them that their breaks are mandated and necessary.

"We want to make sure that all of our customer service associates have their required breaks. It is important that you have uninterrupted rest periods during your shifts. We want the team to be in top form, so we can provide our customers with excellent service."

3. The Security Office

Unfortunately in today's society there are people that we consider to be "non-customers." This is a part of our world and we must train new employees to have an awareness of the role that security plays in your business.

Introduce them to the loss prevention team and show them where they reside. If you have a camera system, show it to them. Your security team protects your associates and your customers.

"I want to introduce you to our loss prevention team and show you where the security office is. Our security team works diligently to provide all associates and customers with a safe environment. We believe in being open and honest with our customers as well as our customer service associates. Having security ensures that we are able to do just that."

4.   The Selling Floor

This is the world that you provide your customers with. This is where they live. Give your new associates a general layout of the store. Explain the importance of the world!

"This is where it all happens! This is the world that we provide to our customers. As members of our team you will assist in providing this world to each and every customer. It is important that we present our world in an organized, neat and friendly environment. We want our customers to be comfortable, we want them to be able to find what they are looking for, we want them to be able to navigate through the store, and we want them to have fun doing it. Everything that you do for our customers will impact the world that they shop in!"

5. **The Front End**

This is a HUGE area of importance! This is the first thing your customers see when they walk through the door. This area should be impeccable! And as you are standing in the front of your establishment you should be hearing your customer service associates speaking with customers. It should sound almost like singing as they greet each person that walks through the door. And when they are ringing through a customer's transaction, there should be a conversation. Is this what you are showing your new employees? And what are you telling them as you stand their proudly at the entrance to your building.

"This is the most important piece of our customer service equation! The register area is at the front of the store, so is therefore the

customer's first impression. This is where we can immediately acknowledge the customer as they enter the store. We can immediately impact how their shopping experience will go today. It is also where they pay for merchandise before their exit. The register area is also their last impression. This is our chance to make sure the customer knows that we appreciate them. This is not only the WELCOME but it is also the THANK YOU!"

As you are conducting the tour, you need to also be showing the new employees that you live what you are speaking. You are the first example of providing excellent customer service that they will see. As you are passing customers you need to be saying "Hello." You need to be smiling. If you are walking around with a group of new employees and you haven't once greeted a customer, then you are showing them that you don't really mean what you are saying. Play the part. Impress your team. Show them the culture from the second you step onto the selling floor! By the end of the tour there should be NO question that the most important thing they do as one of your employees is to provide excellent customer service every single shift!

The orientation has wrapped up! You have all of the new hire paperwork, your new associates have watched a welcome video or taken an on-line training module, and you have toured your team through the store. But most importantly you have successfully introduced them to your customer service culture. End your day by summarizing what you have accomplished together as a new team!

Give each employee their new training schedule.
Never end the orientation without the next step being
planned and scheduled for them. You want them to
engage to your culture and the new team that they are
working with. You need to ensure that they feel
welcome and you need to ensure that they feel
important.

*"Congratulations! You have taken your first step
towards becoming one of our customer service
associates! I want to thank you all for being excellent
students and would like to provide you with your
training schedule! I look forward to seeing you
again."*

Chapter Three

Training means teaching!

Your bright shining stars have just completed their orientation and now it is time for their second shift. This is when you begin to teach them the operational aspects of the business. When your new customer service associates show up for their training shift you should be prepared. The worst thing you can do is have a new employee walk through the doors and you didn't even know they were coming. If you do this you have just screamed at the new employee that they are not important. Make sure you are ready, organized and prepared for their arrival.

Have your new employee scheduled to be with a veteran staff member. The veteran should be a person that you would want representing your customer service culture. Ideally you should already have identified people that you consider expert trainers, in your building. The trainers should be your best! They should be enthusiastic. They should be some of your best producers. They are cheerleaders for your customer service culture! Make sure they are the ones that will be teaching your bright shining stars! They need to mentor your new team members. And you need to facilitate that relationship.

Your new associate should never be left alone during their first shift with your company. You want them to feel safe and secure as they learn. You should never rely on a new associate's training shift for coverage in your building. They haven't learned anything yet. The training you provide should never be considered "throwing them to the wolves." Don't overwhelm them. Your new employee is an investment. You have already spent money on hiring them; don't set them up to feel so overwhelmed that they run for the door! Not only would you be losing a new Customer Service Associate but you'd be losing money!

Have a plan in place for how you will be teaching your new customer service associate every aspect of their new role with your company. Schedule them to learn their role in stages that will make sense and ensure that each stage focuses on the importance of customer service. The amount of time that they spend on each stage will be determined by the size and volume of your business. If you are a big box retailer you may need to devote each stage to an entire four hour shift. If you are a low volume store you may only need one hour on each stage. Nonetheless be organized!

Stage One – The Register

You told your new employee that the front of your building is the most important part of your selling floor during the orientation. This is the first and last impression that your customer gets. If it's the most important aspect of your culture then you need to begin the training there. Every single person that you hire you will develop as a master at the POS station. Every single person that you hire needs to be available to assist at the front end during a rush of business. There should be no such thing as hiring people to just clean fitting rooms or fold shirts. Everybody needs to be an expert in every aspect of your customer service culture. Don't be caught unprepared and in a situation where you have multiple people in the building but only half of them can help in a rush of business.

The operational training of the register system is the easy part. This should certainly be a large part of the training, because the new associate needs to operate the machine. But as they are being taught how to push keys and navigate through the POS system, you should be teaching them the number one focus. They need to be customer service experts! This should be the prime focus of their front end training. And your trainer should be focusing on this!

The POS transaction is a relationship with your customer. The relationship should be looked at as a package full of surprises. Your customers are being given this beautiful package that's pretty and tied up with a big bow on top! When they open the beautiful package they need to be thrilled with the contents.

This is the last chance you have! The customer is leaving. This is the grand finale opportunity to WOW your customer! You want them to come back! Teach your new customer service experts how to present your customers with a **G.I.F.T.**

1. **G**reet

    Smiling and saying "Hello," is the best way to make a customer feel comfortable. You are showing them that you are happy that they are there. You are showing them that you care about them. A customer should be greeted the same way you would greet somebody coming to visit you in your home. They should feel welcome. They are not an interruption of your work they are the purpose of it!

2. **I**nvite – Every single customer, every single time should receive an invitation! The

invitation can take on many different forms but nonetheless they should receive an invitation. The invitation is an invitation to return. It is a reason for the customer to come back again. We want them to come back! This is the chance to invite them to the next party you are sponsoring in your store! The invitation can be a coupon, it can be signing them up for a store credit card, signing them up for an email newsletter account, an announcement for an upcoming sale, or it can be anything at all. Don't let your customers leave empty handed! Appreciate that they are giving you their hard earned money and reward them for that gesture.

3. Feedback – There needs to be a conversation! A transaction should never be silent. Ask the

customer how everything went. Customer's love to give you their opinions! Let them know that what they think matters. There may have been a problem and this is your chance to find out what it was so you can correct it. You may never know if you don't ask. And it can be a simple, "How was your shopping experience today?"

4. **T**hanks – Be appreciative that the customer is supporting your business. Tell them that you enjoy the fact that they came into the store today and handed you some of their hard earned money. Everybody loves to be recognized for something they have done well. The customer is a person too! Recognition at its finest includes a thank you. Thank them!

Stage Two – Talk to the Customer

Your new customer service expert has been taught how to operate the register and how to present your customers with a GIFT, but that's not the only place you should be talking to your customers. There's a whole bunch of stuff that happens before the customer reaches the POS stations. They are shopping, navigating, making decisions, and maybe even struggling before they reach the front end of the store. Some customers may be in your building for over an hour before making their purchases. That's a lot of time being spent in the store. And that's the opportunity that you have to "talk to the customer."

Schedule your new employee with a veteran staff member to learn how to "talk." Your new employees need to be comfortable approaching customers. They can't be shy! And if they are, you dropped the ball during chapter one. Your new associate should spend at minimum one hour being taught how to talk to your customers. During this part of the training they should be on the move. They should be walking through the store with their mentor and they should be approaching customers. The approach can be an offer for assistance, an invitation to sign up for the email newsletter, an offer of a coupon, or an open ended greeting. Open ended greetings can include:

"How are you today?"

"What is it that you are shopping for today?"

"What can we help you with today?"

Some customers might not really want to talk to your new customer service associate and that's okay. You're not looking for the customers to tell you their life story. You're not looking for them to stop shopping and stand in the middle of the store talking with you for an hour. Keep it simple. Be friendly, be inviting, and be genuine. You're not trying to harass your customers but you are trying to tell them that you're available if they need help. Making the customer comfortable is a part of communicating with them. If a customer doesn't respond to your new expert's attempts, tell them to keep moving. Look for the next opportunity.

The point is that your new customer service associates need to be comfortable talking with the customer and they need to know that it is an expectation!

Stage Three – Recovery

How the store is presented to the customer is a HUGE part of the service you provide. The store needs to be neat, organized and clean. Every person in the building should be trained on how to provide this to the customer. It doesn't do any good to have customers in the building if the place is such a train wreck that they are unable to shop!

Have your new customer service expert with a mentor. The mentor needs to teach the new employee the HOWS of recovery in your store. You may have a certain way that you fold the merchandise, you may have a certain way that you present rack/fixture integrity, you may have a certain set of rules regarding fitting rooms; make sure you are teaching your new employees how to properly present the goods to your buying customers.

Beyond the HOWS the mentor also needs to constantly be reminding your new customer service expert of the WHYS. Everything they teach should be presented as a "for the customer" task. The training should include statements such as:

"We need to make sure our customers can find their size, so we put the merchandise in this order."

"When you see tags or trash on the floor make sure you pick it up. We want our customers to focus on shopping, not a mess."

"When we colorize the merchandise it is more pleasing to our customers."

"We should be checking the fitting rooms in between customers. Every customer should have a nice clean environment, so they can be comfortable when they try on the merchandise."

"We put the merchandise back on the shelf as quick as we can so our customers can find what they are looking for."

During the recovery stage the mentor needs to be teaching the new associates how to be operationally good at recovery without taking their eyes off the ball. And the ball is the customer. They need to be taught how to keep looking up! They need to be taught that while they are "fixing" the selling floor, it is still all about helping the customer. Nearly every customer they encounter will have a question. It may be as simple as 'where's the restroom?' but nonetheless they will have a question. The new customer service associate should immediately be using the skills they learned in Stage Two, while they are learning to recover the store.

Stage Four – Let Them Fly

You have taught your new customer service associates how to run the register, how to talk to the customers, and how to recover the store. Now it is time to let them fly on their own! But it's not over yet. Make sure you are still placing them near veteran associates. Your new team members will still have questions, as they continue to learn. Don't expect too much, too fast with your new employees. Schedule them for coverage but place them side by side with people that have the answers. Let them know that it's okay to be asking more questions. Let them know that you expect it. You are still making them understand that they are valuable members of your team. Just because you've trained them on Stage One, Two and Three they are still training for a number of shifts. And this may be slightly different for each candidate. But pay attention to how they are adapting and continue to be available for additional training or refreshers if they need it.

Chapter Four

Who are your leaders and what are they doing?

Your leadership team needs to be the leaders of the experts! And as the leaders they should be the BEST that you have! They are the biggest supporters of the culture and they are the ones that need to ensure that it is consistently in place! Who are your leaders and what exactly are they doing? Are they talking the talk but not walking the walk? They need to walk!

As members of the management team, the leaders have some responsibilities that will take them away from the selling floor. There are certain things and certain tasks that your leaders are responsible for. And your leaders need time to do these things. These things include: Interviews, conference calls, meeting with Customer Service Experts, writing reviews, setting planograms, receiving a truck, planning for upcoming events, etc. There's a lot of stuff that is operational. And these things shouldn't be ignored but they are not the most important aspect of building a customer service culture. The most important thing that you will need to focus on is indeed THE CUSTOMERS! The leadership team needs to not only connect with the customers but they need to manage the culture. We've already established that the front end of the store is the most important area of the store. It's the first impression and the last impression for your customers. There needs to be a leadership presence at the front of the store, every single minute that the doors are open! This is beyond an expectation if you are going to develop a customer service culture; it is the L.A.W.! (**L**EADERS **A**RE **W**ALKING)

Develop a plan that makes sense for your organization. If the store is open for (on average) one hundred hours each week, then you need a leadership presence at the front of the building for one hundred hours per week. Schedule your leaders to manage the culture within the hours that you're open and schedule them for reasonable amounts of time. If your idea of reasonable is four hours, you will have twenty-five blocks of time to fill with a leadership presence. If your leadership team consists of five people, they will each be scheduled for five blocks of time. Five times a week they will be the leaders at the front of the store. Five, four hour shifts they will be leading and managing the customer service culture from the front of the store. That's only twenty hours each week that they will be expected to NOT be in the office, NOT be setting planograms, NOT be doing anything that takes their focus off the most important aspect of your customer service culture: THE CUSTOMER! This still leaves them thirty hours of their fifty hour work week to perform operational tasks. And if your leadership team consists of ten members, they will each be expected to manage the culture from the front of the building for ten hours each week. The latter example would leave them forty hours for the other duties. However the math works out, figure it out, schedule it and deliver it.

Once you have your leaders scheduled to manage the culture, what are they going to do? Are they standing at the entrance like pillars of stone? Are they texting on their telephones? Are they leaning against a fixture? If the answer to any of these questions is yes, you should be evaluating their effectiveness as leaders for your business and reacting. QUICKLY!

So what is the expectation? What are your leaders going to do within their four hour block of time? They're supposed to be managing the culture so how are they going to do that? Think of your leaders as Maestros. They are the conductors of the orchestra. And the orchestra is a big one. There are many people in the orchestra. The orchestra consists of all of your Customer Service Associates. And they are all playing instruments. Some are playing flutes, some are playing trumpets, and some are playing violins. And they are creating music together that your customers are listening to and truly enjoying. And while the music is singing throughout the store, the Maestro is waving his or her arms. Every now and then the Maestro points to just one member of the orchestra and gives specific direction. He waves his arms at varying paces and in various fashions. With every wave and twist and turn and pointing, the Maestro keeps the music playing. That's what your leaders need to be doing at the front of the store. They are the Maestros!

Now that you can picture it, let's break down the responsibilities of your leaders. The expectation is that they are leading the culture. They are managing the flow of the business. They are ensuring that the customers are the most important things in the building. Your leaders need to be the best that you have. They need to show your customer service associates how to be the best at delivering excellent customer service. The expectation is that they

L.E.A.D: L̲OOK… E̲NGAGE… A̲NTICIPATE… D̲IRECT

1. **LOOK**

What should your leaders be looking for? They should be looking for anything that impacts the culture. This includes every detail! Are we paying attention to our customers? Are we giving the G.I.F.T? Are we cleaning out the fitting rooms? Are all of the shirts unfolded and nobody's recovering them? Did somebody spill something and it needs to be cleaned up? There are a million things that will impact the customer service culture. The leaders of the building need to be LOOKING for all of these things. And the only way to LOOK is to be on the move. Standing like a pillar at the front of the store will not accomplish this. The leader needs to be walking. They need to do a loop through the store on occasion. They need to check the fitting rooms.

They need to watch the customer service associates. And they need to be looking for customers that may need attention. As the leaders LOOK, it should be the busiest part of their day. By the end of the shift, your leaders should be tired. If they're not, they're probably not really LOOKing.

2. **ENGAGE**

Your leaders need to ENGAGE. There are two groups of people that the leaders need to engage. They need to engage with the customers and they need to engage with the associates. They should be talking, constantly. They should be greeting the customer and asking them open ended questions. They should be smiling! And they should be the best that you have at engagement. The leaders should be so good at engaging customers that the Customer Service Associates can learn just from watching them in action. As the leaders move through the front of the store they should be taking engagement to the next level. The engagement that they provide should be beyond a smile and greeting. They should be interacting. The leaders need to have a few tricks up their sleeve that will immediately engage a customer. Here are a few tricks:

- Compliment – When the leader sees a customer walking across the front of the store that is not smiling, they should take it as a challenge. One of the best ways to get somebody to smile is to pay them a compliment. And it can be as simple as, "I love that jacket. Did you buy that here?"

- Group Greetings – Quite often, customers come in as a group. Greeting a group will often cause the members of the group to immediately break into conversation. "Hello Ladies! How's everybody doing today?"

- Acknowledge the Children – When you say hello to a toddler that's shopping with Mom, Mom will immediately smile just because the child waves at you. You have greeted the Mom through the child and you've made her smile at the same time.

Engagement needs to include the customer service associates, as well. The leader needs to ensure that the culture is in place. They should be talking with associates and asking them how things are going? If one of your company's expectations is that your Customer Service Associates open three charge accounts per shift for the customer, the leader needs to be paying attention to those goals. They should be driving the numbers through their engagement with the team. They should be asking questions, providing solutions, and helping the Customer Service Associates to deliver the results.

3. **ANTICIPATE**

The leaders need to be anticipating the needs of the customers. As they are moving through the store and looking, they also should be anticipating customer needs. The needs can include additional associates to the POS stations, additional associates to help empty fitting rooms, or shifting of teams throughout the store for recovery. The leader needs to know that when all the carriages are gone from the front end, they are going to need extra people to the front of the store any minute. The leader needs to know that when a mother of two is carrying a large box to the register, she will need carryout assistance. The leader needs to know that if there's a line of customers waiting to go into the fitting rooms, then additional customer service associates will be needed to clean the fitting rooms. The leader should be reacting to these things proactively so the customer is not negatively impacted. Anticipating needs will ensure that the culture remains in place.

4. **<u>DIRECT</u>**

Part of LEADing is directing the Customer Service Associates. As the leader looks, engages and anticipates, they will need to direct associates to assist customers. The leader should be holding a daily line-up (schedule) in their hand as they are on the move. They should have a thorough knowledge of who is in the building and who is available for specific customer needs. When a customer asks for assistance at the back of the store, the leader should immediately inform the customer that they will be sending an expert to meet them. They should know the team, react to customer requests, and direct the team by use of a radio system or paging system; whichever your company provides. They are leading the orchestra here and they need to direct in order that the associates can deliver the culture at all times.

Chapter Five

What do they WANT?

You've hired the team, you've trained them, and you are ensuring that there is a strong leadership presence at the entrance and exit of the store. With these pieces in place have you ensured that the customer's needs are being met? Is it working yet? How do you know? You don't know the answer to this question yet. The only way to really know if a customer service culture is in place is to ask. You need to actively engage the customers and ask them for feedback. When you invite customers to give you an opinion, they will take advantage of it ninety-nine percent of the time. The customer is the best resource a retail environment has for figuring out if their efforts are succeeding.

Establish a forum for soliciting feedback from your customers. Make it a part of the daily routine. Keep it simple. Keep it direct. And be consistent with the requests for feedback. Your leaders are already scheduled for shifts at the front of the store. Your leaders are the perfect people to solicit feedback from the customers. Your efforts to engage customers for feedback will not only get you details of how your culture is succeeding but it will also ensure that leadership is engaging your customers on a daily basis. Instruct your leaders to ask three simple questions, three times per shift:

1. *How is your shopping experience going today?* This question is almost the same as saying hello. It is a greeting but it has a purpose. Are the customer's having a positive shopping experience or are they frustrated? If

things are not working for the customer, you

now have an opportunity to react.

2. *Were our associates helpful?* You are training

your customer service associates to be

available and considerate of customer's needs.

Asking this question will tell you if the

training and mentoring is working. Leaders

can't be in every corner of the building at all

times throughout the day. There are things that

may be happening within the departments that

the leaders just aren't seeing. Asking

customers this question will keep leaders

aware if the customer service associates are

doing their job.

3. *If you could change one thing about our*

service what would it be? This question is the

big one. This is a wide open ended question

that will give you specific feedback. A customer may tell you that they would change nothing! And this is great feedback that you can appreciate and relish in. But the customer might tell you that they are furious because as hard as they shopped and as much time as they have spent in the store, they simply cannot find a single shirt that is their size. This is feedback that you can immediately react to. Not only can the leader assist the customer that is already frustrated but they can react and ensure that additional sales will not be lost.

What good is asking questions if you aren't listening, though? As you gather information from your customers, you will be able to react to some. The responses that you receive will dictate how immediate your response needs to be. But there may be feedback that will take efforts and time to react to.

You may hear from customers that they would get more shopping carriages for customers. You can react to this immediately by sending an employee to the parking lot for retrieval. But if you need to order more carriages it will be a number of weeks or months before you receive them. You may hear from customers that they would suggest more assistance in the shoe department. You can immediately send additional staff to that corner of the building. Whatever the responses are the important things are that you are asking, you are listening and you are responding.

Chapter Six

ONE WORD – RECOGNITION!

You've hired your team of customer service associates, you've brought them through orientation, and you've trained them. They have the tools they need to succeed. Now you need to watch them. How are they doing? Are they utilizing the tools that you have provided or are they stumbling? The only way to know that your new associates, and veteran associates for that matter, are delivering the service results is to observe them. You need to watch and you need to recognize. The biggest recognition associates receive is that you have given them a job. But that's not enough! People like to hear that they're doing a good job as they continue to learn and grow with the company they work for. If you have trained them and now you are walking away, you are telling them that their performance is not really that important to you. You need to stay in touch and encourage them to improve their performance if necessary. If they are doing a great job you need to tell them. You need to reward the great results that your customer service associates deliver through a detailed recognition program.

There are a variety of ways to recognize the team and the great performances. You are building a culture of excellent customer service! The recognition needs to focus on the culture! The recognition needs to focus on excellent customer service! If everything your customer service associates do is already tied to the culture, then so should the recognition program. Make sure you are constantly reminding your associates that their performance positively impacts customer service. Remember to praise associates efforts but reward the results! Keep three things in mind as you develop a recognition program that your associates will engage to. <u>Remember the FOUR 'C's</u>:

1. <u>C</u>REATIVE – Be creative! Keep it fun but keep it simple. Throughout the work day there are many things that your associates are responsible for. Come up with different ways to keep them surprised, engaged and having a great time providing the service culture. You can play "musical envelope" and as associates open company charge accounts for customers, the envelope is passed from associate to associate. At an undisclosed time you announce that whoever's holding the envelope wins what's inside! You can reward associates

with candy as they assist customers with carry-

outs! You can reward associates with an extra

fifteen minute break for every hand-written

positive customer comment regarding their

performance. You can do anything at all!

Keep it simple and keep it fun!

2. CEREMONY – There's much to be said for

public recognition. Post photos on a bulletin

board for the customer service associates of the

month, appoint a customer service leader to

organize the ceremonies, make announcements

at morning or evening huddles. Make sure

your associates are hearing the success stories.

Not only will the ceremonies inspire associates

to improve their performance, so they can be

recognized too, but it will also publically

recognize the results that others have delivered.

3. CONTESTS – People tend to be very competitive! People love to win! As your creative juices are flowing come up with contests that will keep the associates fighting for results and the recognition that goes with it! You can hold raffles for a prize and every entry to the raffle is rewarded as associates positively impact customers. Try to shake it up and do something new every month. You don't want associates getting bored with recognition. Keep things changing and keep it exciting!

4. CONSISTENCY! It does no good whatsoever to establish a recognition program for your associates if you are not paying attention to it.

A successful recognition program is one that the leaders are committed to. The leaders are the ones that typically recognize associates so their involvement is key! Commit to your associates, commit to recognizing them, and show them every single day that what they provide for the customers is important!

Chapter Seven

Soliciting GREAT ideas

You've hired your team, you've introduced them
to the company, and you've trained them to deliver.
They are the ones that you trust to be on the front line
with your customers. They're living and breathing
the company's expectations. They are your experts.
So why aren't you asking them what they think?
They have GREAT ideas but you have no forum in
place to gather their thoughts and suggestions. Solicit
great ideas from your customer service associates.

Develop a solicitation program for your team and
gather their ideas. Put a locked box in the break-
room with a sign on it: "Creative Customer Service
Culture Corner"… "Idea Central"… "Any
Thoughts?" Call it whatever you want and encourage

your associates to present their great ideas. Create a customer service culture IDEA form. Make sure you are capturing who, when and what on the form. Keep it simple and precise.

Associates may present an idea that is clearly not going to work. That's okay! Let them think about things. Let them try to creatively enhance what you are delivering to your customers. It is okay for them to present an idea that just won't work. The important thing is that you've got them thinking. They are engaged to the culture and they want to be a part of the culture. It's all good news!

You've gone to the trouble of creating a form for soliciting customer service culture ideas, you've set up a corner or a box for gathering the ideas, now what are you going to do once you have a nice little stack of ideas in front of you? Read them! Don't ignore the team's efforts. See what your associates are saying and see what they've come up with. There could be and probably will be some awesome suggestions!

Every associate that makes a suggestion should be recognized. This recognition can be a simple thank you during a morning huddle or it can be a small token of appreciation. The important thing with recognizing the associates' efforts is that the entire team sees that you are taking notice, you are reading their suggestions, and you are encouraging all associates to get involved. If the associate's suggestion is ACTED on, there should be an even greater reward! Maybe the associate who makes an awesome suggestion gets to park in the best parking space for one week. Maybe that associate gets to have a month of Saturdays OFF. Whatever you come up with for a reward doesn't have to be expensive but

it should be a big deal!

Chapter Eight

COMMUNICATE!

There are literally dozens, hundreds, maybe even thousands of 'things' that happen every single day in a retail environment which impact customers. Some of these things won't require daily communication but some of these things will. What are you doing to ensure that your associates are informed? You've made the hires, you've trained your customer service associates, you are recognizing them and encouraging their involvement but what are you telling them? Keep them informed! They need to know what's going on in the building. They need to know what specials are being offered to the customers. They need to know if systems have been updated. They need to know if the hours are being extended through an upcoming holiday weekend. There are so many details that can get lost in the shuffle at in a busy retail environment, how are you going to ensure that every single associate is being informed?

Imagine the negative impact to your customers if your associate comes into work, hops onto a register and immediately start cashing out a customer. And just as the transaction has been completed the customer asks about the twenty-five percent savings coupon that they should have received. The associate looks innocently at the customer and asks, "what savings coupon?" Now the customer gets to stand around impatiently while the associate calls a manager for help, has the transaction voided and re-rung, and fumbles with multiple receipts and apologies. All of your efforts to create a culture were just torpedoed. You need to make sure that your customer service associates are informed. Don't send them to the front line until you have ensured they receive the necessary tools to do their job effectively! And how are you going to do this? Here are three modes of communication to ensure that you are reaching each customer service associate:

1. **DAILY MEETINGS** - Hold quick informative meetings at the opening, the middle and closing of each business day. Gather all available associates and let them know what is going on. (This is also an opportunity for some recognition too!) This meeting is a daily overview. But be quick and be painless. Don't keep your customer service associates standing around for a forty-five minute dissertation. You will lose the crowd. Keep the daily info

meetings to a quick five minute overview. Encourage your associates to get to work quickly, so they can assist more of your customers! Keep the meeting positive! You are preparing your experts for their day, which you want filled with smiles, engagement, and the culture. Get them ready for the day and get them excited for the day!

2. **NEWSLETTER** – What's going on, what's coming up, what's over? Each week your associates should receive some notice about what you are offering to your customers. This notice can be as simple as one piece of paper that is left for each associate to pick up and read. This can be a responsibility that you give to one of your customer service leaders, a veteran staff member, an assistant manager,

whoever you want.   If you don't want to go

through that much paper, keep it even simpler

and create a poster board or an easel board that

tells the associates what the week ahead looks

like. The point is that the customer service

associates need to be informed.

3. **DETAILS** - A CUSTOMER SERVICE

COMMUNICATION BOOKLET - This can be

as simple as a wide-ruled spiral notebook and a

pen, sitting on the table in a break-room or

open office area. The booklet is to be used for

communicating DETAILS to the team. The

booklet is to be used by the associates and for

the associates. The booklet is a communication

vehicle for daily details and information

regarding the customer service culture.

Associates should be encouraged to read the

entries and initial that they have read them.

Entries may be:

"We have a large piece of furniture being held for a customer on the loading dock; they'll be in tonight to pick it up; the furniture has been paid for."

"A lost wallet was found and is locked up in the office; if a customer calls, forward them to the manager."

"One of our stores in Alaska is trying to find item-X for a customer; the item is sold out company wide. Should we get one of these items as a return, please let the manager know."

Make sure you are being thorough as you communicate with your customer service associates. They need to be informed for the

customers! They need to be prepared for the

day! They need to represent the service

culture!

Chapter Nine

HOW BIG OF A DEAL IS IT?

How big do you want the culture to be? Whether you are a single location or multiple locations, you need to ask yourself this question. How big is big enough? Do you want to ensure that your business is breathing, living, and strengthening the customer service culture through their associates every single second of every minute of every hour every day? If your answer is YES, then you need to make it BIG!

Most companies roll out recognition ideas, contests, directives, new procedures, new measurements, and a host of things that will promote and encourage positive customer experiences. They require that the leaders within each location are supporting the recognition programs. They define clear expectations of what customer service needs to look like. And all of these things are good things. And it's important that things like this do happen within an organization. But these things alone will not bring your customer service culture to the next level. What will bring the culture to the next level?

The strongest, most effective, and BEST customer service culture extends beyond the four walls of the business. It starts at the very TOP! What are the TOP LEADERS of your company doing to ensure that an EXCELLENT CUSTOMER SERVICE CULTURE exists? What are they doing that is beyond the norm? What are they doing that's so out of the box fantastic, that there's no way you cannot ensure that an excellent customer service culture exists within the framework of each and every retail location that your company has? It's okay if you can't come up with an answer to this question. I'm going to give you one.

You've hired your customer service associates. You've taken your new team through orientation and you've trained them. You are leading by example. You are talking to your customers. You are recognizing your associates. You are encouraging involvement. You are communicating with your team. Now what? What else? What will bring this all home and SCREAM to your associates that you mean what you say? You need to make it BIG!

Each person that works for the company will know that the number one thing they do is provide customers with excellent customer service. They will each know that the culture is a requirement. They will each know that you mean what you say. They will know that their efforts are working. They will know that they are appreciated. They will know this because you are going to recognize and reward the BEST of the BEST within your culture of excellent customer service!

Announce to your entire organization that you recognize the BEST customer service leaders, throughout the organization, on a yearly basis. Roll out the biggest recognition program that your company offers and MAKE IT BIG! You need to come way out of the box on this one. You need to show the entire organization that you are serious about building a culture. How are you going to do this? What is it going to look like? Create an award program that spans the entire organization and focuses on delivering excellent customer service!

THE HIGHLIGHTS:

- THE BEST OF THE BEST RECOGNTION PROGRAM

  - Delivered yearly!

  - Anybody can win!

- ANYBODY can nominate ANYBODY!

  - Undetermined number of winners!

BREAK IT DOWN:

1. Announce it. Send a poster to each location, hold a conference call, and put it on the internal web-site. Whatever method you chose, just be exciting! You are announcing to the entire company that you are rolling out the biggest award program you have ever offered. Make sure they get the message!

2. Provide forms. Tell your associates that they (anybody) can nominate whoever they feel

delivers the best customer service. Encourage them to tell the story. Encourage them to provide details. Each form will require the associates full name, employee ID number, and location. Each form will have enough space that the nominator can tell you why they are nominating the person that they are.

3. Gather the nominations. All of the nominations will need to be sent to a central location, probably at corporate headquarters, where they will be organized alphabetically. Create binders. (you may need more than one binder)

4. Form a committee. You will need a number of committee members, from various locations throughout the organization. You want to make sure that you have representatives from every

department: stores, distribution centers, human resource department, loss prevention, etc.

5. Require that each committee member reads each nomination. They will want to flag nominees as "maybe" and "yes" as they review. Guide your committee members to get to a reasonable amount of worthy nominations. When they are done reviewing they might have ten, twenty or fifty potential winners. The amount will depend on the original number of nominees and the size of the organization.

6. Meet as a committee to review the top choices. Each committee member will get the opportunity to speak about individual nominees. And at the end of the meeting(s) the committee will vote for the winners! The vote

MUST be unanimous. There can be any number of winners!

7. Make the announcements. Tell the entire organization who the winners are! And make the announcements as big as the recognition program! Make the announcement as big as the award. Make a trip to where the winners are and shake their hand. Solicit a member of the TOP of the organization to find the winners. Is the CEO available? Fly to wherever you have to go and find your winners!

8. RECOGNIZE THEM at a CEREMONY! Have a celebration! Rent a performing art center and put each winner up on stage! Present a video introduction on the big screen telling everybody who the winners are and what they have done to support the customer service culture!

9. GIVE THEM A PRIZE! How about one-
thousand dollars each? How about a week's
paid vacation? How about a package of prizes?
Make it BIG means recognize it BIG!

This is the grand finale of your excellent customer
service culture! This will show every single associate
that you are serious. You mean what you say.
You're talking and you are walking. And you
appreciate them and all that they do for the
customers!

Chapter Ten

MEASURE IT!

Did it work? And how are you going to know if it did? Establish tools for measuring the results. You need to see that your efforts are paying off. You can do this through:

- OBSERVATION

  Your leaders are already at the front of the store and they are LOOKing. Your customer service associates are delivering excellent customer service to your customers. But what are the customer's doing? Are they storming out of the store with anger? Are they all smiling and making purchases? Watch them and continue to ask them how their shopping experience has gone.

- SURVEYS

  Many companies rely on customer service surveys and surveys are an excellent tool for measuring customer service results. If you already have a survey program in place, you're ahead of the game. If you don't, make the investment and GET ONE! This is a consistent means for gathering information and anonymous feedback from your customers.

  If funds are extremely limited, you as one of the leaders, can ask a neighboring store manager to "shop" your culture. Let them know what you want to have in place with your culture and ask them to visit your location.

There are many ways to gather information from your customers, or business partners, to ensure that your culture is consistently in place. The important thing is that you directly measuring results through specific feedback from your customers.

- SALES

With an excellent customer service culture in place, sales will go up! If your customer service associates are truly engaged and your customers are truly happy, you will see the results through an increase of sales. Ensure that you have a good basis for comparison and measure results across multiple departments, compared to the existing plan, and last year's numbers.

- RECOGNITION RESULTS

  Do you have one of the company's best customer service associates working in your building? Are you finding enough reason and examples to recognize your customer service associates every single day? If these things are happening, you're doing it! You're teaching, encouraging, engaging, and rewarding your associates!

SUMMARY

Congratulations! You've finished reading all about how to build a customer service culture in a retail environment! Now the fun begins! Now you get to put your plan into action, engage your team, and deliver the results! You have the tools and you know what steps you need to take. Let's recap:

- Hiring the Team of Experts!
- The Orientation is the Overview
- Training Means Teach!
- Who are your leaders and what are they doing?
- What do they Want?
- One Word: RECOGNITION
- Soliciting GREAT ideas

- COMMUNICATE

- How big of a deal is it?

- Measure it!

Ten easy steps and you are on the way to building a customer service culture within a retail environment. You have a plan and now you need to deliver it! It is time to commit to your plan.

Be the leader that you are! Encourage your team! Be enthusiastic! And above all else be consistent. You have the tools, you've hired the team, you've taken the steps and you are now ready to deliver the results!

"BUILD A CUSTOMER SERVICE CULTURE IN A RETAIL ENVIRONMENT!"

I know you and your teams will be completely

amazing and would love to hear your stories of

success!

EJBones@outlook.com

Or

EJ Bones@EJBones1 (via Twitter)

Wishing you the greatest success!